Sunflowers

by Gail Saunders-Smith

Pebble Books

an imprint of Capstone Press

1

Pebble Books

Pebble Books are published by Capstone Press
818 North Willow Street, Mankato, Minnesota 56001
http://www.capstone-press.com
Copyright © 1998 by Capstone Press
All Rights Reserved • Printed in the United States of America

Library of Congress Cataloging-in-Publication Data
Sunflowers/by Gail Saunders-Smith.
  p.cm.
  Includes bibliographical references (p. 23) and index.
  Summary: Simple text and photographs depict the
life cycle of the sunflower, from seeds to sprouts to
flowers that finally turn again to seeds.
  ISBN 1-56065-489-9
  1. Sunflowers--Juvenile literature. 2. Sunflowers--
Life cycles--Juvenile literature. [1. Sunflowers.] I. Title.

QK495.C74S335 1997
583'.99--dc21
                    97-23580
                    CIP
                    AC

Editorial Credits
Lois Wallentine, editor; Timothy Halldin and James
Franklin, design; Michelle L. Norstad, photo research

Photo Credits
Phillip Roullard, 8
Unicorn Stock/Jeff Hetler, cover, 14; Tom Edwards, 3,
    4, 20; Dede Gilman, 6; Deneve Feigh Bunde, 10;
    Martha McBride, 1, 3, 12, 18; B.W. Hoffmann, 16

Table of Contents

Sunflowers come
from seeds.

6

Sunflower seeds
become sprouts.

8

Sunflower sprouts
become stalks.

Sunflower stalks
become buds.

Sunflower buds
become sunflowers.

Sunflowers grow.

Sunflowers grow
and ripen.

Sunflowers ripen
and make seeds.

Sunflower seeds
make sunflowers.

Words to Know

bud—a small growth on a plant that turns into a blossom

grow—to increase in size

ripen—to age until ready to eat

seed—a part of a plant from which a new plant can grow

sprout—a young plant that has just appeared above the soil

stalk—the long main part of the plant from which the leaves and flowers grow

sunflower—a large flower with yellow petals and a dark center

Read More

King, Elizabeth. *Backyard Sunflower.* New York: Dutton Children's Books, 1993.

McDonald, Mary Ann. *Sunflowers.* Plymouth, Minn: The Child's World, 1996.

Parker, Philip. *The Life Cycle of a Sunflower.* New York: The Bookwright Press, 1988.

Internet Sites

I Love Sunflowers
http://www.sunflowergal.com/sunflows/sunflow.htm

Sunflowers
http://www.sunflowers.com/index.html

Virtual Garden
http://www.pathfinder.com/
@@zRYn3QYAFesKS17x/vg

Note to Parents and Teachers

This book illustrates and describes the life cycle of a sunflower. The text and photos enable young children to understand how one stage of development leads to the next. The clear photographs support the beginning reader in making meaning from the text. Children may need assistance in using the Table of Contents, Words to Know, Read More, Internet Sites, and Index/Word List sections of the book.

Index/Word List

Word Count: 35
Early-Intervention Level: 6